CHASING GOLD

Centenary of the British Olympic Association

THE IMPORTANT THING IN THE OLYMPIC GAMES IS NOT WINNING BUT TAKING PART. THE ESSENTIAL THING IN LIFE IS NOT CONQUERING BUT FIGHTING WELL.

BARON de COUBERTIN

CHASING GOLD

Centenary of the British Olympic Association

Nick Yapp

gettyimages®

CHASING GOLD

First published in the United Kingdom by British Olympic Association,
1 Wandsworth Plain, London SW18 1EH

This book was produced by Getty Images, 21–31 Woodfield Road, London W9 2BA
Fax 44 (020) 7266 2658

This publication is intended as a celebration of British Olympic history. It is not and does not purport to be a complete record of British Olympic participation or success. Whilst all care has been taken in the collation of the information contained herein, the British Olympic Association is not responsible for any errors, factual or otherwise.

ISBN 0-901662-02-X

Editor **Mark Fletcher**
Designers **Tea McAleer, Vivienne Brar**
Picture Researcher **Jennifer Jeffrey**
Production Manager **Mary Osborne**

Printed in England by Butler & Tanner Ltd, Frome

(*Page 1*) Alison Williamson on target at Athens 2004.

(*Page 2*) The Olympic torch enters Wembley Stadium, London for the 1948 Games, 29 July, 1948. The scoreboard misquotes de Coubertin, who said, 'The honour is less in winning than in taking part... '

(*Page 6*) HRH Princess Anne prepares to take part in the Three Day Equestrian event at the Montreal Games 1976.

(*Endpapers*) Members of Team GB's victorious crew celebrate winning gold in the Men's Eight at the Sydney International Regatta Centre during the 2000 Olympic Games.

Contents

BUCKINGHAM PALACE

As President of our National Olympic Committee, the British Olympic Association, it gives me considerable pleasure to introduce *Chasing Gold* which has been produced to mark the historic milestone of our Centenary.

The British Olympic Association was founded on 24th May 1905 in the House of Commons and has since been responsible for managing over 10,000 of our country's finest sportsmen and women at the Olympic and Olympic Winter Games every four years.

We take pride in our position within the Olympic Movement being one of only three countries which has had athletes compete at every Olympic and Olympic Winter Games. We are also proud that we have always raised all the necessary funds to run the organisation, including the costs of sending Team GB to the Games, from commercial sponsorship and fundraising.

Over recent years we have expanded our role to provide vital services to potential Olympic athletes, and their governing bodies, over the entire four year cycle of the Olympiad. We must continue to meet the ever increasing demands of high performance sport in the 21st Century if we are to remain competitive in the most demanding of sporting environments, the Olympic Games.

I hope you enjoy *Chasing Gold* which beautifully records some of Team GB's greatest Olympic moments over the last 100 years.

Anne

1896 ATHENS
1900 PARIS
1904 ST LOUIS

In 1890, Baron Pierre de Coubertin visited the little town of Much Wenlock in Shropshire. He had come to meet a local GP, Dr William Penny Brookes, founder of the Much Wenlock Games some 40 years earlier. In the early days, the annual Games included wheelbarrow races, pig-chasing, and old women racing for a pound of tea, but by the time of de Coubertin's visit, they were true athletic festivals, with a mixture of track and field events. The Baron was so impressed that he took the idea back to France, where he presented it as his own. The Ancient Games of Olympia were to be revived, and the sports field was to replace the battlefield as an arena for international rivalry. There was initial opposition. Some regarded the idea as 'a faked antique', but in 1894 delegates from 12 countries met at the International Congress of Paris and agreed to re-establish the Games. Two years later, the Olympics returned to Greece.

The Athens Games attracted competitors from 14 nations, among them John Pius Boland, a tennis player who arrived a mere spectator, and left as Britain's first Olympic champion. He borrowed kit and racquet to win two silver medals (there were no gold medals in the early Games). The man he beat in the final was Dionysius Kasdaglis – a fellow amateur, and the man who had lent him the racquet. It was a foretaste of the true Olympic spirit.

For all its idiosyncrasies – some events were open only to members of the Greek Navy – the First Olympiad was a staggering achievement and a huge popular success: 100,000 spectators crammed the stadium for the Marathon finish. There was immediate competition among cities seeking to host the next Games. Some campaigned to keep the Games permanently in Athens, but de Coubertin wished to join the 1900 Olympics to the Exposition Universelle Internationale, to be held in Paris. Four years later, eager lobbying by the United States secured the Games for St Louis, as part of the 1904 World Fair, and the Games became a traveling festival.

Britain won 28 medals in Paris, and produced another double champion in John A. Jarvis. Despite being 'fat all over… with breasts that fell like a woman's', Jarvis won the 1,500- and 4,000-Metre Freestyle events. Perhaps his size gave him an advantage, for all swimming races were held in the Seine, heading downstream with the current, and Jarvis took more current than anyone else. It was a different story for British athletes in St Louis. The Olympic medals for these Games were inscribed: 'ST LOUIS 1904. AMERICA WELCOMES THE WORLD', but most of the world couldn't afford to come, and more than half the events had only American competitors. Of the 252 medals awarded, American athletes won 214. They had tasted glory, and four years later, that seemed to have gone to their heads.

(*Previous page*) Crowds gather for the 1896 Olympics in the Panathinaiko Stadium, Athens, home of the Ancient Games.

MODERN MARATHON Barefoot athletes train for the 1896 Marathon in the countryside around Athens (*left*). A trial Marathon was held in February, but few were impressed with the winner's time of 3:45:00, and so two more trials were held before the Greeks selected their team. Among team members was Spiridon Louis, a shepherd, who became the first modern Olympic Marathon champion, with a time of 2:58:50. (*Above*) Poster for the 1896 Games.

AFTER 1500 YEARS A display of gymnastics in the Panathinaiko Stadium (*below left*) – note the sharp bends on the running track. The Stadium was the home of the Ancient Games. The first International Olympic Committee (*below right*) – standing, left to right: Dr W. Gehardt (Germany), Jiri Guth-Jarkovsky (Czechoslovakia), Francois Kemery (Hungary), and Victor Balck (Sweden); sitting, left to right: Baron de Coubertin (France), Demetrius Vikelas (Greece), and General Alexander de Boutowski (Russia).

MAKING WAVES The start of the 1,500-Metre Freestyle race in the Asnieres basin on the Seine, Paris 1900 (*left above*). The race was won by the redoubtable John A. Jarvis, a house painter from Leicester, and a man with 'powerful shoulders and tremendous thighs'. He may well be making the biggest splash (second from right).

THE GREAT GAME AT THE OLYMPICS
Great Britain beats France 4–0 to take gold in Football at the Paris Olympics, 1900 (*left below*). It was an odd tournament. Three teams took part – the Upton Park Football Club team representing Britain, a team from France, and a Belgian team that included one British player – Eric Thornton. (*Above*) One of the official posters for the 1900 Olympic Games. Sadly, the posters only served to exacerbate some of the confusion as to whether athletes were participating in the Exposition or the Games.

WHITES ONLY Spectators at St Louis (*above right*) were segregated. Many prominent African-Americans called for a boycott of the Games by black athletes, but George Poage and Joseph Stadler insisted on taking part. Stadler won silver in the Standing High Jump, with a leap of 1.45 metres, second only to the great Ray Ewry (1.60 metres), affectionately known as 'The Human Frog'. (*Above*) A poster advertising both the 1904 St Louis Games and the World's Fair in the same city. The design, with its 'fish-eye' lens view of the city was also used as the cover for the programme of the Games.

WAITING FOR THE GUN Runners get set for the Final of the Men's 400 Metres in St Louis, 1904 (*right*). The course was only three-quarters of a lap long, but there were 13 entrants and no lane markings. A degree of chaos ensued. Note George Poage (10th from left), one of the first two black athletes ever to compete in the Olympics, and one of the first to pick up a medal – he took bronze in the 400-Metres Hurdles.

1908 LONDON
1912 STOCKHOLM

William Henry Grenfell, Baron Desborough, was Britain's own de Coubertin and a sportsman of intense energy. Desborough had scaled the Alps, twice swum Niagara, hunted big game from the Rockies to the African veldt, and been President of the MCC. He was also a huge admirer of the work of de Coubertin and his International Olympic Committee (IOC). In the spring of 1905, Desborough threw all his enthusiasm into the founding of the British Olympic Association, and the first meeting was organized by Howard Vincent MP, a member of the IOC since 1901. The BOA was to have one main aim – to organize British teams for all subsequent Olympics.

The IV Olympiad had been scheduled for Rome, but funds were not available, so the 1908 Games came to London. The BOA got to work. 'The Great Stadium' was built on wasteland to the north of Shepherd's Bush, and London prepared to welcome 2,467 competitors from 22 nations. Just before the Games opened, the Bishop of Central Pennsylvania preached a sermon in St Paul's in which he said of the Olympics: 'The important thing... is not so much to have been victorious as to have taken part.' De Coubertin was present in the Cathedral, and a few days later, he borrowed the Bishop's words: 'The most important thing is not to win but to take part, just as the most important thing in life is not the triumph but the struggle. The essential thing is not to have conquered but to have fought well.' The Olympic Spirit was born.

It was an awkward baby, prone to tantrums. The weather was foul throughout the London Olympiad, and bad temper led to them being dubbed 'The Battle of Shepherd's Bush'. After their sweeping successes in St Louis, some American athletes and officials approached the London Games in a swaggering frame of mind, and British reaction was at times ungenerous. There were disputes and disqualifications, protests and provocations, rows and re-runs. Most athletes shrugged their shoulders at the vicissitudes of a sporting life, but both during and for months after the Games a war of words raged in journals and newspapers, with accusations from US officials of taunts, abuse of their flag, unsportsmanlike conduct, and even cruelty. Bogus interviews in magazines reported bogus referees making bogus admissions that they had failed to report British 'cheating'.

After all this, Stockholm hosted the pleasantly peaceful Fifth Olympiad in 1912, its organization praised by all and with no ugly scenes. Britain took 41 medals in all, with gold in both the Men's and Women's 4 x 100-Metre Relay, Soccer, the Rowing Eights, the Small Bore Rifle, the Women's Singles, and Mixed Doubles at Tennis, and a superb victory for Arnold Jackson in the 1,500 Metres. And everyone looked forward to the VI Olympiad at Berlin in 1916.

(*Previous page*) Ben Jones, British winner of the 5,000 Metre Track Race at the 1908 London Olympics.

ROYAL OPENING Edward VII arrives at the newly-built Great Stadium for the opening of the London Olympics (*left*), 27 April, 1908. Within moments of his arrival, the Battle of Shepherd's Bush had begun. Infuriated by the absence of the American flag from the others decorating the stadium, US flag bearer and discus champion Martin Sheridan refused to dip his own Stars and Stripes as he passed the King's box. 'This flag dips to no earthly king,' he said. Sheridan, a New York City policeman, broke the Olympic discus record a few days later to add yet another gold medal to those he had won at St Louis in 1904 and at the unofficial Intermediary Games in Athens 1906. (*Above*) Programme cover for the 1908 London Games.

A BEVY OF BRITISH BOXERS – all of whom won gold medals at the 1908 Olympics: (*far left*) Henry Thomas (bantamweight); (*left from top to bottom*) Albert Oldham (heavyweight); Richard Gunn (featherweight), at 37 the oldest fighter ever to win an Olympic championship; and J. W. H. T. Douglas (middleweight), known to cricketers as 'Johnny Won't Hit Today' Douglas. As well as being a boxer, Douglas was a painfully slow scoring batsman who captained Essex and England.

VICTORY LAURELS British and American wrestlers hold their Olympic wreaths (*above*). To judge from the size of the wrestlers, they are probably (from left to right): George Mehnert (bantamweight), George de Relwyskow (lightweight), George 'Con' O'Kelly of Ireland (heavyweight), Stanley V. Bacon (middleweight), and George Dole (featherweight).

ONE MAN FINAL There were four contestants in the 400-Metre Final, run on 23 July. Three were American runners, the fourth and favourite was Wyndham Halswelle of Great Britain (*above on right*). As the athletes approached the last bend, some 30 metres from the tape, John Carpenter moved to his right, obstructing Halswelle. There was a spontaneous howl of disgust from many spectators and judges held up their hands, calling 'foul' and 'no race'. British and American officials and athletes invaded the track (*left*) and it took 30 minutes to restore order. Carpenter was disqualified and a rerun ordered. The other Americans refused to take part and Halswelle ran on his own, to take gold. He was so upset by the affair that he immediately quit sport. Halswelle was killed by a sniper on the Western Front, 31 May, 1915.

THE LONG BOW OF OLD ENGLAND

Women archers (*below*) compete in the National Round competition, won by Queenie Newall (*opposite, third from left*), then 53 and still the oldest woman ever to win an Olympic medal. (*opposite, far left*) Beatrice Hill-Lowe, winner of bronze in the National Round. (*opposite, centre*) William Dod, gold medal winner at the London Games. (*Right*) William's sister, Lottie Dod, who won silver. Lottie was a phenomenal athlete – archer, skater, Wimbledon champion, cricketer, and the first woman to attempt the Cresta Run at St Moritz. She and William were descendants of Sir Anthony Dod, who commanded the English archers at Agincourt in 1415.

GOLD ON LAND AND WATER Henry Taylor (*left*), the cotton-mill worker who won gold in the 400-Metre Freestyle in 1908. (*Top*) The City of Liverpool Police Tug-of-War team dig in their heels to pull their opponents from the USA. Two months later, at a banquet in the States, James E. Sullivan, Secretary to the American Olympics Committee, accused them of wearing special boots. It was an unjust accusation but yet another broadside in the Battle of Shepherd's Bush.

FOUNDING FATHER Boater in hand, and with Lady Desborough to his right, Lord Desborough (*above*), President of the BOA, addresses spectators at the rowing events at Henley. Among his other positions, Desborough was an MP, Master of Draghounds, Mayor of Maidenhead, Chairman of the Thames Conservancy Board, and a man who loved fine whisky.

HAPPY LANDINGS Cornelius 'Con' Leahy of Dublin (*below*) practises for the High Jump. He won silver in London, clearing 1.88 metres. Harry Porter of the USA won the gold medal, and for a while it was rumoured that the American jumpers were being supplied with a magic liquid by their coaches. One French athlete smuggled a sample of the liquid to a pharmacist for analysis. It turned out to be water.

THE PLAN THAT FAILED Theodore Just (*right*) qualifies for the Final of the 800 Metres. Just and Ivo Fairbairn-Crawford hatched a plan to exhaust the American favourite, Melvin Sheppard. From the start of the Final, Crawford set a cracking pace, to take Just away from Sheppard, but the plan didn't work. Sheppard caught and passed Just, Crawford dropped out of the race, and Just finished in fifth place.

NATURE'S GRANDSTAND Spectators await the arrival of runners in the 1908 Marathon. In the background is Wormwood Scrubs, the largest prison in Britain. The Marathon route ran alongside the gaol's perimeter wall, and it was rumoured that 'good conduct men' would be allowed on the wall to watch the runners pass. They weren't.

THE NAKED POLICEMAN George Larner (*left*), a member of the Brighton Constabulary, crosses the finish line to win gold in the 3,500-Metre Walk, 14 July, 1908. He gave unusual advice on training: 'When circumstances permit, all clothing should be removed for a run round a secluded garden, especially if it is raining at the time.'

JUST REWARD Larner, in suit with head bowed, collects one of his two gold medals at the London Games (*above*). His other victory was in the 10-Mile Walk, staged for the first and last time in the history of the Olympics at the 1908 Games.

A HAPPIER GAMES Professor Olle Hjortzberg's multi-flag design for the Stockholm Olympics poster 1912 (*left*). Two British gymnastics team members in action on the horse (*below*). The 23 man team won a rare Gymnastics medal for Britain at the V Olympiad, taking bronze in the Team Combined Exercises.

OLYMPIC GAMES
⌐ STOCKHOLM 1912 ⌐
JUNE 29 th — JULY 22 nd.

TOP TEAMS The winning British Water Polo team (*top left*) at the Stockholm Olympics. Britain took gold at this event in every Games from 1896 to 1920. The British Women's 4 x 100-Metre Freestyle team (*below left*). Second from the left is Jennie Fletcher, a mill girl from Leicester who worked a 12 hour day, six days a week, and trained when possible in the evenings.

STRIDING JACKSON (*Above*) Arnold Jackson of Great Britain sets a new Olympic record of 3:56:8 and wins the 1,500 Metres. Abel Kiviat of the USA (third from left) and Norman Taber (extreme right) were respectively second and third, but it needed the first ever use of a photo finish camera at the Olympics to reveal this. Jackson, who preferred to train by playing golf, walking, and having daily massages, later became more famous as Arnold Nugent Strode-Jackson, the youngest ever Brigadier-General in the British Army. Kiviat was to become, at the age of 91, one of the torch bearers for the 1984 Olympics in Los Angeles.

1920 ANTWERP
1924 PARIS CHAMONIX
1928 AMSTERDAM ST MORITZ

Tragically, the world reverted to the mayhem of the battlefield and there was no VI Olympiad. When the guns finally stopped firing in 1918, the problem was where to hold the 1920 Games. Europe was exhausted. Old empires had been dismembered by war and revolution. International mistrust choked the air. Eventually, Antwerp was selected. It was appropriate that the Phoenix of the Olympics should rise from the country that had suffered most in the War.

Against the wishes of de Coubertin, Germany, Austria, Hungary, Bulgaria, and Turkey were banned from the Games, as aggressors in the war, but 29 nations took part. The Olympic Flag flew for the first time, and the Athletes' Oath was introduced. Ice hockey made its first appearance, tug-of-war its last. The diving events were held in a moat, in water so dark that divers became disoriented. Britain's winning water-polo team were attacked by Belgian spectators and had to be protected by armed guards. Great Britain won 42 medals, 14 of them gold – only the USA and Sweden did better. There were gold medals for the Men's 4 x 400-Metre Relay team, for the Tug-of-War team, for boxers Ronald Rawson (Heavyweight) and Harry Mallin (Middleweight), for Harry Ryan and Thomas Lance in the 2,000-Metre Tandem Cycling, for the Polo and Water Polo teams, for the Men's and Women's Doubles in tennis, and for the 7-Metre Class Sailing team. Percy Hodge won gold for Britain in the 3,000-Metre Steeplechase, and then gave hurdling displays at which he cleared jumps while carrying a tray, a bottle and full glasses – without spilling a drop.

The Games returned to Paris in 1924 for the VIII Olympiad. Here the Olympic motto was first adopted – Citius, Altius, Fortius (Higher, Faster, Stronger). Perhaps 'Bigger' could have been added, for the Games now attracted 44 nations. On the whole this was a friendly Games, though a French boxer named Brousse was disqualified for biting Britain's Henry Mallin. It was claimed that Brousse had a habit of snapping his jaws when he threw a punch, and that Mallin had bumped his chest against Brousse's snap.

An Olympic innovation, also against the wishes of de Coubertin, was International Sports Week 1924, held at Chamonix and later recognized as the first of the Olympic Winter Games: 18 nations and 418 competitors took part. The British team won a silver and two bronze medals, a considerable achievement for a nation that could rarely train for winter sports at home. A second Winter Games was held in St Moritz in 1928, and Amsterdam was the venue for the Summer Games, with 4,000 competitors, including 360 from Britain. The feeling was that Britain, with only 20 medals (three gold) should have done better. The problem for all nations, however, was that as the Games expanded to include more and more nations, competition became increasingly fierce, and winning became harder.

7ᵉ Olympiade. Anvers 1920.
...filé Les Athlètes (G.de Bretagne)

VIIᵉ OLYMPIADE
ANVERS (BELGIQUE)
AOUT-SEPTEMBRE 1920

(*Previous page*) The Olympic rings (representing the five major land masses of the world) make a fashionable appearance at Longchamps, Paris 1924.

FAST TRACK TEAM (*Opposite*) British athletes at Antwerp. Among them are Guy Butler who won silver in the 400 Metres (back row, second from left); Harold Abrahams (back row, third from left); and Harry Edward, who won bronze in both the 100 and 200 Metres (sitting, right). Other track medal winners at the Antwerp Olympics included Philip Baker, who won silver in the 1,500 Metres and later, as Philip Noel-Baker, was awarded the 1959 Nobel Peace Prize, and Percy Hodge, who won gold in the 3,000-Metre Steeplechase – despite having to stop, remove a shoe, adjust it, and replace it.

PARADE OF THE ATHLETES (*Above*) The British team march into the Olympic Stadium at the start of the Antwerp Games, 14 August, 1920. The ceremony included, for the first time, the Olympic Oath, taken by Victor Boin on behalf of all athletes: 'I promise we shall take part in these Olympic Games, respecting and abiding by the rules which govern them… in the spirit of true sportsmanship, for the glory of sport and the honour of our teams.' (*Left*) Poster for the Antwerp Games.

LONDON EXPRESS Albert Hill (*above*), a 31-year-old railway guard, receives an illuminated certificate from his employers, in recognition of his double gold medal successes in the 800 and 1,500 Metres at the Antwerp Games. In the 1,500 Metres, Hill was accompanied for most of the way by Philip Baker, who ran alongside him to protect him from strategic challenges and won the silver medal. Like many athletes, Hill's best years had been spent at war. He served in the trenches and in the Royal Flying Corps.

TWENTY-A-DAY MAN Hill wins the 800-Metre Final (*right*), with Edgar Mountain, also of Great Britain, in fourth place. Hill was trained by the redoubtable coach Sam Mussabini, who later coached Harold Abrahams, but Hill may not have taken his training all that seriously. He claimed that his major preparation for the Antwerp Games had been to cut his cigarettes down to 20 a day.

THE OLYMPIC SALUTE One of the Hachard posters (*above*) for the 1924 Paris Games. The sale of souvenir merchandise such as posters, badges, lapel pins, postcards, stamps, medals, and even coasters has raised money for every Games since 1896.

FIRST DEFEAT ON WATER A water polo game in progress (*left*) at the Olympic Pool, Les Tourelles, 16 July, 1924. This was the first modern Games in which Britain failed to win this event. In this pool Johnny Weissmuller of America won three gold medals at the Paris Olympics. Five years later he signed a contract with BVD Swimwear, Los Angeles, and in 1932 he was swimming in his first Tarzan film.

46

TRIPLE GOLD (*Left, top to bottom*) Harold Abrahams hits the tape and wins gold in the 100 Metres, Paris 1924. His time was 10.6 seconds and it was the third time he had equaled the Olympic record in 26 hours. After winning the 800 Metres, Douglas Lowe receives congratulations from Paul Martin of Switzerland who came second. Eric Liddell takes Britain into the final of the 4 x 400-Metre Relay. He missed the final itself, as it was held on a Sunday.

THE PRINCE AND THE SPRINTER (*Opposite*) Edward, debonair Prince of Wales, adjusts his hat as he speaks to Harold Abrahams after the first round heat of the 200 Metres, Colombes Stadium, Paris, 8 July, 1924. Abrahams finished sixth in the 200-Metres Final. Before the final of the 100 Metres, he had said that he felt 'like a condemned man just before he goes to the scaffold'.

THE FIRST OLYMPIC WINTER GAMES

British skaters (*opposite top*) prepare for
the Chamonix Games, 16 January, 1924 –
(from left to right) B. H. Sutton, L. H.
Cambridgeshire, and A. E. Tibbet. They were
unplaced. (*Below far left*) Favourites for the
Women's Figure Skating at Chamonix: (left to
right) Herma Planck-Szabo (Hungary/gold),
Ethel Muckelt (GB), and Beatrix Loughran
(USA/silver). Ethel Muckelt took bronze,
becoming the first British athlete to win a
Winter Games medal. There was also bronze
for the British Ice Hockey team, and silver for
Ralph Broome, Thomas Arnold, Alexander
Richardson, and Rodney Soher (*above*) in
the Four Man Bobsleigh. (*Left*) The poster for
the Chamonix Games of 1924.

THE LEAPING LORD David George Brownlow Cecil Burghley (*above*) on his way to winning the 400-Metre Hurdles Final, Amsterdam 1928. Burghley had been off-colour in the semi-final, finishing only third. In the final, however, he ran making 'every hurdle a winning post' and equalled the Olympic record of 53.4 seconds. For the race, his mother supplied him with special silk shorts, that were very soft and prevented chafing of the legs.

THE DEFENDING CHAMPION Following his success at Paris in 1924, Douglas Lowe (*far right*) again takes gold in the 800 Metres at Amsterdam, setting a new Olympic record of 1:51:8. His main rival had been Otto Peltzer of Germany, but Peltzer suffered an injury and was eliminated in the semi-finals. After the final, Lowe sent him a charmingly sympathetic letter. (*Right*) One of the posters for the Amsterdam Games. The tower featured on many posters, including those of the LNER, advertising train and boat connections to the Games.

EARLY CONTENDERS (*Left above*) Muriel Freeman of Great Britain (back to camera) takes on Helene Mayer of Germany in the final of the Women's Foils, 2 August, 1928. Freeman won silver in what was the only Women's fencing event in Amsterdam. (*Left below*) Alf Baxter of Great Britain completes his lift in the Men's Weightlifting, 30 July, 1928. Although Launceston Elliot won two weightlifting medals at the 1896 Athens Olympics, over 50 years were to pass before Britain had other successes in this discipline, when Julian Creus won silver in the Featherweight class and James Halliday won bronze in the Lightweight class at London in 1948.

TRIUMPHANT OARS The British Eight (*above*) raise their oars in celebration of their victory over Italy on the Sloten Canal, Amsterdam, 3 August, 1928. They went on to win a silver medal. Among them is Jack Beresford, winner of rowing medals at five successive Olympics from 1920 to 1936. His father, the British rowing coach, Jack Beresford Senior, described the water at Amsterdam as being 'practically dead'.

SKELETON BOB (*Left*) The Earl of Northesk and Jennison Heaton (USA) prepare for the Skeleton Bobsleigh run at the St Moritz Olympic Winter Games, 11 February, 1928. Captain L. M. Boddam Whetham of the St Moritz Tobogganing Club reported that 'owing to Colonel Moore-Brabazon's unfortunate accident, Great Britain was left with no second string, and therefore Lord Northesk had to carry the whole weight on his shoulders.' The Earl took bronze.

OLYMPIC CAN-CAN Competitors in the Women's Figure Skating at St Moritz take time out to perform an unofficial ice dance (*above*). Though the Opening Ceremony for the Games was marred by 'one of the worst blizzards ever experienced', subsequent conditions and arrangements were an improvement on those at Chamonix four years earlier. (*Left*) One of the official posters for the 1928 Olympic Winter Games at St Moritz.

1932 LOS ANGELES
LAKE PLACID
1936 BERLIN
GARMISCH-PARTENKIRCHEN

The 1932 Summer and Winter Games were held at a time of deep economic depression. Understandably, the BOA decided not to send a British team to the Winter Games in Lake Placid – though a few hardy British competitors made their own way. Further, the BOA sent only competitors who had a real chance in the finals to the X Olympiad in Los Angeles. The journey from Britain to California was slow and expensive. It involved five days at sea, and five more on the railroad from Toronto, with a stop for a few hours in Albuquerque, where athletes managed to have a shower and take a walk.

In Los Angeles they found excellent facilities and the first purpose built Olympic Village. The Games ran smoothly, with the exception of the 3,000-Metre Steeplechase. Officials lost count of the number of laps the contestants had run, and the race became the 3,460-Metre Steeplechase, the extra lap allowing Tom Evenson of Britain to overtake McCluskey of the USA and gain silver. The British team did well, winning 16 medals, among them four gold, and there would have been another gold had it not been for the honesty of Judy Guinness in the Women's Foil. In the final, she pointed out that the judges had missed two 'hits' scored by her opponent, Ellen Preiss. Perhaps the most remarkable British success was that of Thomas Green in the first Olympic 50-Kilometre Walk. Born with rickets, Green hadn't walked at all until he was five. When he was 12 he had lied about his age and joined the Army. In the War, as well as being gassed, he had been wounded three times. His was a hard won gold medal.

Organisation of the 1936 Berlin Games was faultless. The comfort, catering, and facilities of the Olympic Village surpassed anything Los Angeles had offered. The Reichssportsfeld took the breath away. The stadium was a tour de force. But there were problems: the Nazi attitude to the American 'black auxiliaries'; the reception given at the March Past to the British, and others, who did not give the Fascist salute; the knowledge that so much evil lurked in the shadows. For a long time, it was touch and go whether Germany would be allowed to host the XI Olympiad.

The Comte de Baillet-Latour, de Coubertin's successor at the IOC, paid a visit to Germany early in the year to inspect arrangements for the Winter Games in Garmisch-Partenkirchen. He came across a sign outside the toilet block on the Olympic site: 'DOGS AND JEWS ARE NOT ALLOWED'. The Comte protested. This was not in conformity with Olympic principles. 'When you are invited to a friend's home,' said Hitler, 'you don't tell him how to run it.' 'When the five-circled flag is raised over the stadium,' replied the Comte, 'it is no longer Germany. It is Olympia and we are masters there.' The signs were removed.

(*Previous page*) Mickey Mouse gazes down on a heat of the 110-Metre Hurdles in the Coliseum Stadium, Los Angeles during the 1932 Games.

ALL FOR WINNIE (*Above*) Thomas Hampson breaks the tape ahead of Alexander Wilson of Canada, to win gold and set a new world record in the 800 Metres. He attributed his victory to his fiancée, Winnie. 'A world beater must be inspired,' he wrote, 'and what greater inspiration can anyone have than the love of such a beautiful, kind, gentle, sweet, good creature.' (*Left*) Samuel Ferris takes silver in the 1932 Marathon. The winner, Juan Carlos Zabala of the Argentine, struggled across the line 19 seconds ahead of Ferris, who was still full of energy.

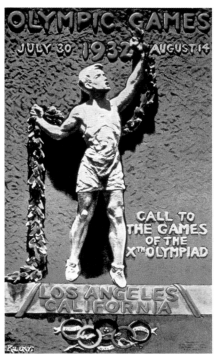

LONG DISTANCE HERO (*Left*) Eileen Hiscock (on left) and Violet Webb flank Tom Green as the *Empress of Britain* berths at Southampton, 26 August, 1932. Green was a late starter in sport, entering his first walking contest at the age of 32, yet won the 50-Kilometre Walk in Los Angeles six years later. (*Top*) The official Olympic poster for the Los Angeles Olympics. 'Smokey' (*above*) was the official mascot of the 1932 Games and was born in the Olympic Village.

MILITARY PRECISION A fleet of limousines, reserved for VIPs, waits outside the Olympic Stadium, 30 July, 1936 (*left*). The organization of the Games was faultless. Every event began on time. Every athlete had the finest training facilities. The construction and running of the Olympic Village was the responsibility of Captain Wolfgang Fuerstner, a half-Jewish officer in the German Army. On the last night of the Games, having completed his work, but knowing what was to come, Fuerstner shot himself.

FLAME FROM OLYMPIA The runner for the final leg of the torch relay lights the flame in the Lustgraten, Berlin, 1 August, 1936 (*inset*). The flame had left Olympia 12 days earlier, and had travelled via Athens, Salonika, Sofia, Belgrade, Budapest, Vienna, Prague, and Dresden to Berlin. It arrived only 10 minutes late, when the torchbearer ran into the stadium, halted, raised the flame above his head, and plunged it into the bowl. (*Above*) One of the series of posters by Wurbel for the Berlin Olympics 1936.

(*Previous pages*) Leslie Southwood (left) and Jack Beresford rest their oars after winning the Double Sculls at the Berlin Olympics, 1936. Beresford won rowing medals at every Games from 1920 to 1936.

BEATING THE BLIGHTERS (*Far left*) The British gold medal 4 x 400-Metre Relay team: (left to right) Arthur Brown, Frederick Wolff, Godfrey Rampling, and William Roberts. Their approach to training was casual. 'Look here, chaps,' said Rampling, 'we really ought to practice some baton changing.' They did, became bored and 'packed it in', but were still convinced they could 'beat the blighters'.

LONG DISTANCE MEN Harold Whitlock (*above right*) bustles through the last few metres of the 50-Kilometre Walk at the Berlin Olympics. Whitlock had no coach and trained alone. After 30 kilometres there was no glucose drink available, so he drank tea sweetened with condensed milk, which made him sick. He kept going and won gold, beating the previous Olympic record by 20 minutes. Ernest Harper (*above left*) took the silver medal in the Marathon, though he finished in desperate pain from a blister that had filled one of his shoes with blood.

GOLD, SILVER, AND BRONZE The Olympic Winter Games at Garmisch-Partenkirchen were the most successful ever for Britain. Fifteen-year-old Cecilia Colledge (*opposite*) won silver in the Women's Figure Skating, coming second to the great Sonja Henie. The British Four Man Bobsleigh team (*top right*) won bronze. (*Top left*) A poster for the Garmisch-Partenkirchen Games.

UNDEFEATED (*Above*) A scrabble near the goal as the British ice hockey team defeat Sweden on their way to a gold medal, breaking the Canadian total domination of this event since 1920 in Antwerp. Great Britain beat Canada in the semi-final and held out against the United States in the final.

1948 LONDON ST MORITZ
1952 HELSINKI OSLO
1956 MELBOURNE CORTINA

The world went to war and there were no were Games in 1940 or 1944. The Olympic Torch was not relit until 1948, when it was brought to Wembley for the XIV Olympiad. Germany and Japan were banned from the Games, but 4,099 competitors from 59 nations came to a London still reeling from the Blitz, still tightening its belt against food rationing, and still under austerity regulations. This time there was no purpose built Olympic Village. Athletes were housed in schools and Army camps, and there were complaints – mainly from the Press. But the weather was glorious, and Sigfrid Edstrom, President of the IOC, had nothing but praise for the BOA's organization: 'It was a challenge to the British genius for improvisation, and the organization rose gloriously to the supreme challenge.'

Britain won only three gold medals, but there was plenty of silverware. John Wilson and William 'Ran' Lawrie won gold in the Coxless Pairs, despite the fact that until 1948 they had neither of them touched an oar in 10 years. Richard Burnell and Bertie Bushnell rowed their way to gold in the Double Sculls, Stewart Morris and David Bond sailed to gold in the Swallow Class. And there were near misses. Timekeepers could not separate the times of Maureen Gardner and Fanny Blankers-Koen's in the 100-Metre Hurdles. The Men's Hockey team reached the final, but lost to newly-independent India. And for three days, following a temporary disqualification of the United States team, Britain held 4 x 100-Metre Relay gold. Britain had one shining star in the Winter Games – Jeannette Altwegg won bronze in the Women's Figure Skating at St Moritz in 1948. Four years later, Altwegg won gold.

The 1952 Summer Games were held in Helsinki. For the first time, the British team flew to the Olympics, but the Games were a disappointment. Britain had its lowest medal count since St Louis in 1904 – one gold, two silver, eight bronze. The hero of the hour was Harry Llewellyn's 'Foxhunter', leaping to gold in the Equestrian Team Jumping on the very last day of the Games. Sheila Lerwill, then the World Record holder, came second in the Women's High Jump, and Charles Currie took silver in the Olympic Monotype Sailing Class. Shirley Cowley held the Olympic Long Jump Record for approximately one minute. Kenneth Richmond, better known as the man who beat the gong at the start of every J. Arthur Rank film, won bronze in the Super Heavyweight Wrestling.

Melbourne in 1956 was a happier time. Though there were two boycotts (that by Egypt, Iraq and Lebanon over the Suez Crisis; that by Spain, Switzerland and the Netherlands against the Soviet invasion of Hungary), over 3,500 competitors from 67 nations took part. Britain had its best Games since 1924, taking gold in Athletics, Boxing, Swimming, Equestrian events (held in Stockholm because of Australian quarantine laws), and Fencing.

(*Previous page*) Athletes and officials march down Olympic Way, Wembley for the opening of the London Games, 29 July, 1948.

WEMBLEY HEAT WAVE Spectators at Wembley Stadium (*left*) do their best to protect themselves from the sun during the London Games, 14 August, 1948. Save for one day of torrential rain, the Games were held in a heat wave, with temperatures in the 90s each day. (*Above*) The official poster for the London Games, showing the classical statue of Discobolus against a background of the Houses of Parliament. At the statue's feet are the five Olympic Rings.

PHOTO FINISH The final of the 100 Metres in the Wembley Stadium, 1948 (*left*). The sprinters are (right to left) Harrison Dillard (gold), Barney Ewell (silver), Lloyd la Beach (bronze), Alistair McCorquodale of Great Britain (4th), Melvin Patton (5th), and E. McDonald Bailey of Trinidad (6th).

A CLOSE CALL (*Above*) Maureen Gardner (extreme right) leads in one of the heats of the 80-Metre Hurdles, 3 August, 1948. In the final, Gardner took silver, recording the same time as Fanny Blankers-Koen of the Netherlands. The band immediately struck up the National Anthem, and Kohn thought Gardner had won. But the band were playing simply because the royal family had just arrived.

A WALK IN THE SUN Terence 'Tebbs' Lloyd-Johnson (*far left*) takes bronze in the Final of the 50-Kilometre Walk. Then aged 48, Lloyd-Johnson remains the oldest athlete ever to win an Olympic Track and Field medal. He missed silver by only 14 seconds, but John Ljunggren of Sweden, the winner, was seven minutes ahead.

LONDON OLMPIANS Three of the British team at the London Games 1948 (*left, from top to bottom*): Edna Childs, British springboard diving champion who came 6th in the Olympic finals; Donald Scott (right) in action against de Segni of Italy – Scott won silver in the Light Heavyweight class; and Reg Harris (seen here winning 'Sportsman of the Year' 1950), who won silver medals in both the 100-Metre Cycle Sprint and the 2,000-Metre Tandem, with Alan Bannister.

THIRTY MILES TO GO. H.S. Bignall (*above right*) lights a new torch for the Olympic Flame in Redhill, Surrey, 28 July, 1948. Ahead lies London – where petrol rationing left the streets virtually clear of traffic for the runners.

MIXED FORTUNES Britain's Four Man Bobsleigh team of William Coles, William McLean, R. W. Pennington Collings, and George Holliday (*far left*) prepare for a practice plunge. They came seventh. John Crammond (*above left*), winner of the bronze medal in the Bob Skeleton event at St Moritz, 1948. Conditions were mixed at St Moritz that year, and Colonel Evan Hunter, the BOA Chef de Mission, described the ice as having the quality of a 'sheet of marzipan'. (*Left*) The official 1948 Winter Games poster.

ICE CHAMPION Jeannette Altwegg (*above right*) takes bronze in the Women's Figure Skating, February 1948. Altwegg was British champion from 1947 to 1950, European champion in 1951 and 1952, and World champion in 1952. At the Oslo Olympic Winter Games in 1952 she won gold in the Figure Skating event with a performance that was described as 'the embodiment of accuracy'.

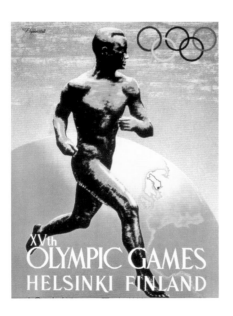

HOPES DASHED Emil Zatopek leads the field in the final of the 5,000 Metres (*top left*). Behind him are Alain Mahmoun of France and Herbert Schade of Germany, while an exhausted Christopher Chataway falls after hitting the track kerb. Chataway finished fifth, one place behind Britain's Gordon Pirie. Zatopek won the 5,000 Metres, the 10,000 Metres, and the Marathon. (*Below left*) Roland Hardy strides out in the final of the 10,000-Metre Walk. Moments later, he was disqualified for 'not walking properly'. He was one of six athletes disqualified in the heats and the final, and the controversy that followed led to the event being dropped from the Olympic calendar.

'FOXHUNTER' TO THE RESCUE As the Helsinki Games neared their end, Britain had yet to win a gold medal. Success and relief came when Harry Llewellyn, captain of the British equestrian team, completed the team's performance in the Prix des Nations on 'Foxhunter' (*above*). The horse became a national hero, and its skeleton was subsequently preserved by the Royal College of Veterinary Surgeons, but the gold medal win had been set up by Wilfred White on 'Nizefella' and Douglas Stewart on 'Aherlow'. (*Left*) The poster for the Helsinki Olympics.

THE REAL THING After training on grass at home, Hilary Laing hits real snow in the Swiss Alps near Davos, January 1952. She was one of a team of seven British skiers practicing for the first Women's Cross Country event in the Oslo Games of that year. (*Inset*) The poster for the Oslo Olympic Winter Games 1952.

VI OLYMPIC WINTER GAMES
14-25. FEBRUARY **OSLO** NORWAY 1952

A GOLDEN HANGOVER Chris Brasher (*left*) hits the water in the Final of the 3,000-Metre Steeplechase at the Melbourne Olympics, 29 November, 1956. He was first across the line, but was then disqualified. On appeal, he was reinstated as the winner, but by then it was too late for him to receive his medal that day. He celebrated throughout the night, was still drunk with joy and tonic when he stepped on to the winner's podium the following morning. (*Top left*) Judy Grinham with the medal she won in the Women's 100-Metre Backstroke. (*Below left*) Terry Spinks, winner of the gold medal in Flyweight Boxing. Two hours before the final, it was discovered that Spinks was a pound and a half overweight. He skipped for half an hour in a hot room. (*Top right*) The poster for the Melbourne Games. (*Below right*) The poster for the equestrian events, held in Stockholm because of Australian quarantine laws.

1960 ROME SQUAW VALLEY
1964 TOKYO INNSBRUCK
1968 MEXICO CITY GRENOBLE

The Swinging Sixties brought us the Beatles, Che Guevara, Martin Luther King, the Mini, and the mini skirt. The Olympics kept on growing, ever more competitive, ever more expensive. The BOA needed to raise £50,000 to send the team to Rome, £180,000 for Tokyo in 1964, and £175,000 for Mexico City in 1968. The 1960 Summer Games in Rome were hailed as the biggest, the best, and the most spectacular of all time, though it was here that the spectre of drugs first raised its ugly head. Knut Jensen, a Danish cyclist, died after injecting himself with amphetamines and nicotinyltartrate. The intense publicity surrounding the Games now led to their being used as a platform for political protest. Shortly before the 1968 Games opened in Mexico City, 250 people were killed when students demonstrated against the extreme disparity between rich and poor. A few days later, Tommie Smith and John Carlos rocked the sporting world when they gave the Black Power salute from the winners' podium following the 200-Metre Final.

There was a more scientific approach to training and the effects of weather on performance. Don Thompson trained for the 50-Kilometre Walk in Rome by filling his bathroom with heaters and steaming kettles, sealing the doors and windows, and exercising in conditions that replicated those of a Roman September. Lynn Davies was blessed by the Welsh gods who produced Welsh weather in Tokyo for his gold medal winning Long Jump leap. Mexico City posed a problem for almost all athletes, with the Games held 2,300 metres above sea level. It was predicted that there would be 'those that die'. The BOA sent a research team of six distance athletes, a coach and two doctors to Mexico to explore conditions. One of the athletes, Martin Hyman, reported: 'If I had my heart set on an Olympic medal, I would give up my job one year before the Games and take another one at a similar altitude to Mexico City.'

Though it was true that more athletes than usual needed oxygen after track events in Mexico, no one died. Paul Nihill collapsed 44 kilometres into the 50-Kilometre Walk. He was put in ambulance and treated for exhaustion, then recovered sufficiently to eat a light meal in the evening. At midnight, he was found wandering round the Village, incapable of sleep. At 2AM he was pouring out his story in a letter to his wife.

Britain had little success in either the 1960 Winter Games in Squaw Valley or those in Grenoble in 1968, although British athletes competed in all sports save ice hockey. There was triumph at Innsbruck in 1964 for the Two Man Bobsleigh team, but also horror at the accidental death of Kay Skrzvechi while practicing for the Luge event. And in 1971 Lillian Board, one of Britain's most promising athletes and winner of the silver medal in the Women's 400 Metres at the Mexico Games, tragically died of cancer.

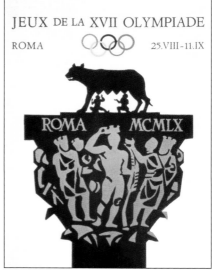

(*Previous page*) Spectators congregate in the shadow of one of the 60 statues surrounding the Olympic Stadium in Rome, 1960. The statues, commissioned by Mussolini, were condemned as indecent by the Italian Church.

THE TEAM TAKES TO THE AIR Members of the British Olympic team prepare to board a BEA Viscount for their flight to Rome, August 1960 (*left*). With one exception, a competitor who was allergic to air travel, all team members and officials went by air, and in those days travelled en masse. There was no system of staggered departure and arrival, based on the different length of time each discipline needed for practice and acclimatization, and a fleet of aircraft was needed – Comets, Viscounts, and one Britannia. (*Above*) An official poster for the Rome Games.

TWO IN THE AIR, TWO ON THE GROUND
(*Clockwise from top left*) Don Thompson heels-and-toes his way over 50 kilometres of Roman way on a clammy evening, 7 September, 1960. Elizabeth Ferris plunges to silver in the Women's springboard. Weightlifter Louis Martin secures the bar before rising to bronze in the Heavyweight section. Mary Rand has a disappointing day in the Long Jump – although favourite for the event, she failed to qualify for the final.

THE PRICE OF GOLD (*Right*) The British Women's team for the 4 x 200-Metre Medley: (left to right) Natalie Steward, Jean Oldroyd, Anita Lonsbrough, and Sylvia Lewis – missing is Sheila Watt. Anita Lonsbrough's great moment came in the 200-Metre Breaststroke, where she won gold and became the first woman to break 2:50 for the event. In some ways it was a costly success, for her employers docked her wages whenever she took time off to train.

THE WINNING LUNGE Giuseppe Delfino scores a winning hit on Britain's Allan Jay to take gold in Men's Individual Epee. Delfino's strategy was to keep on level terms with his opponent until time ran out, then, in the sudden-death overtime, launch a sudden barrage (*left*). It worked at Rome, and Jay had to be content with a silver medal.

A TELLING BLOW Southpaw Dick McTaggart (*above*) leads with his right against Blay of Ghana, 2 September, 1960. Known as the 'Glasgow Ratcatcher' – though he came from Dundee – McTaggart won gold at the Melbourne Olympics and bronze at Rome in the Lightweight class. He remained an amateur for his entire career, and was regarded as one of the most stylish of boxers.

SQUAW VALLEY CALIFORNIA FÉVRIER 1960

LES VIIIème JEUX OLYMPIQUES D'HIVER

A STUDY ON ICE (*Right*) Photographer Ernst Haas's portrait of two skaters practicing for the Women's Figure Skating at Squaw Valley, January 1960. The event was eventually won by Carol Heiss of the United States, who then followed Sonja Henie to Hollywood, but gave up after one film – *Snow White and the Three Stooges*. Britain's most successful athlete at Squaw Valley was Terence Monaghan, who finished fifth in the Men's 10,000-Metre Speed Skating. (*Above*) The official poster for the VIII Winter Olympiad – 57,228 copies of this poster were produced in five different languages.

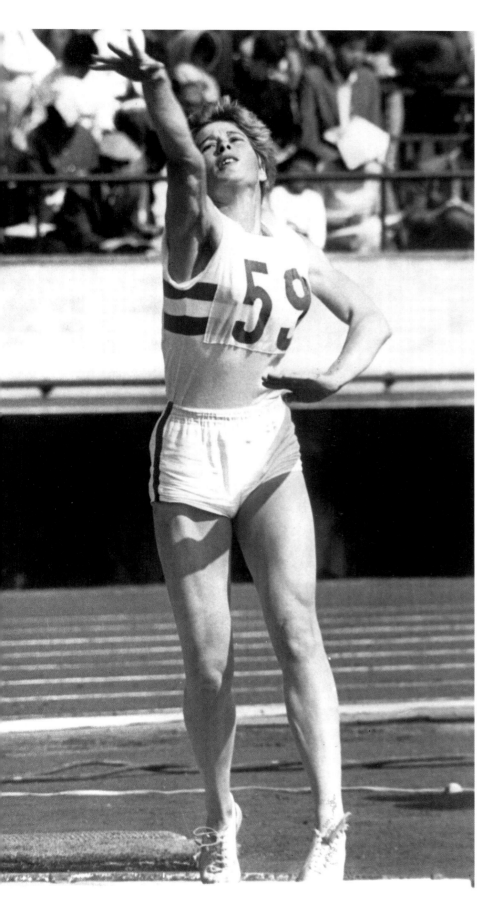

LYNN THE LEAP Reckoned by many the greatest moment in Welsh sporting history – (*far left*) Lynn Davies jumps 8.07 metres to become the Olympic Long Jump champion, 18 October, 1964. He had timed his jump to perfection, waiting to start his run-up until the flags hung limp in the stadium, indicating that the wind had dropped. (*Above*) The famous 'start' poster for the Tokyo Olympic Games.

THE WEAKEST LINK Mary Rand (*left*) in action during the shot put in the Women's Pentathlon, Tokyo, 16 October, 1964. It was her weakest discipline. The eventual winner, Irina Press of the USSR, out-pointed her by 1,173 to 789 in this event, and Rand had to be content with silver. 'I'm pretty dumb about technique,' she said. Mary Peters, whose glory was yet to come, finished in fourth place.

THE LONGEST KISS Sheila Matthews (*above*) waves to the crowd after her husband Ken Matthews wins the 20-Kilometre Walk in a record time of 1:29:34. Sheila broke through the security guards, crossed the track and gave him what is reckoned to be the longest kiss in Olympic history. After the race, and after the kiss, Matthews said: 'My legs hurt me. They still do. But I wouldn't mind going dancing.'

FROM THE JAWS OF DEFEAT Ann Packer (55) acknowledges Betty Cuthbert's victory in the Women's 400 Metres at Tokyo, 17 October, 1964 (*right*). Packer's golden moment was three days later. She had considered not taking part in the 800-Metre Final, and going shopping instead. When her fiancé Robbie Brightwell finished a disappointing fourth in the Men's 400 Metres, however, she changed her mind. 'I was thinking about him and not about myself, and so I wasn't nervous… I was so relaxed, I was able to look up at the electric scoreboard and think "first lap in 58.6 – it doesn't seem that fast".' She won gold.

INNSBRUCK
1964
29.1.-9. 2.
TYROL
AUTRICHE

AFTER 12 YEARS... While Robin Dixon hangs on behind, Tony Nash pilots the British Two Man Bobsleigh team to a gold medal at the Innsbruck Olympic Winter Games, 3 January, 1964 (*right*). It was Britain's first gold medal at the Winter Olympics since Jeannette Altwegg's success at Oslo in 1952. Earlier, Nash and Dixon had broken a bolt on their sled, but Eugenio Monti, a rival in the event, supplied them with a replacement. (*Above*) The poster for the Innsbruck Games.

OLYMPIC IDENTITY, OLYMPIC INDUSTRY
School children play on the giant Mexico68
logo beside a swimming pool (*far left*).
By the 1960s competition to host the
Olympic Games had become intense. One
of the official posters (*above*) for the 1968
Mexico City Games.

LILLIAN'S SILVER Lillian Board relaxes after
the final of the 4 x 100-Metre Relay in
Mexico City (*above left*). Her triumph in the
Mexico Games was to win silver in the
Women's 400 Metres, immediately after
which she began training for the 1972
Munich Games. Tragically, she died of cancer
in a Munich clinic in 1971.

AZTEC GOLD David Hemery (*centre left*)
clears the last hurdle and heads for the tape
and a new world record in the 400-Metre
Hurdles Final, Mexico City. He crossed the line
with an eight metre lead, the largest winning
margin since 1924, but wasn't sure that he
had won until he was interviewed by the BBC.
Chris Finnegan (*below left*) had a similar
problem when he won the Middleweight
Boxing Final. 'We were called to the centre of
the ring for the announcement,' he said. 'At
first I couldn't cotton on to the jabber, but all
of a sudden I heard the magic word that
sounds the same in any language –
FINNEGAN!'

1972 MUNICH SAPPORO
1976 MONTREAL INNSBRUCK

True to form, the XX Olympiad was the biggest yet, with 7,173 competitors from 122 nations. It was the first Games at which there was full scale testing for drugs, and the first at which a single athlete won seven gold medals – Mark Spitz of the United States. But these were violent times – in Vietnam, Chile, Northern Ireland, Nigeria, Cambodia, and many other places – and the Munich Olympics will always be remembered for what happened on 5 September.

Just before dawn, members of the Black September Movement entered the Israeli compound, killed two members of the Israeli team and took nine hostages. Plans to rescue the hostages failed with disastrous results. Here was a grim new crisis for the Olympics. There had long been concern at commercial and political pressure, at boycotts and bans, at the growing problem of 'shamateurism'. Now it seemed that terrorism threatened the very existence of the Olympic Movement, and a new kind of battlefield had replaced the sports field. A memorial service to those that had died was held in the stadium, and 34 hours after the raid began, the Games were resumed.

They were dominated by the Soviet Union, from the giant Ivan Yarygin who pinned all seven of his opponents on his way to Heavyweight Wrestling gold, to the diminutive gymnast Olga Korbut. Britain's stars were more quietly triumphant. Martin Reynolds, Alan Pascoe, David Hemery, and David Jenkins snatched silver by a fifth of a second in the 4 x 400-Metre Relay; Rodney Pattisson and Christopher Davies won a second sailing gold in the Flying Dutchman class; and there were two Equestrian golds, including double gold for Richard Meade. One of the British horses, Cornishman V subsequently embarked on a career in films, starring in *Dead Cert* (1974) and *International Velvet* (1978).

There were no medals for the British team at the Winter Games in Sapporo, Japan in 1972, but four years later, at Innsbruck, John Curry produced a performance so scintillating that he not only won gold, but became a national hero.

Those that had wanted to reduce the size of the Games had their way in 1976 at Montreal – 22 African nations imposed a boycott in protest at a tenuous link between the Olympics and the Apartheid politics of South Africa. The reason given was the inclusion of New Zealand, whose rugby team had recently played the South African Springboks. Though only 88 nations took part in the Montreal Games, the cost was said to be high enough to bankrupt the city for the next 20 years. Among the less successful performances that hit the headlines were those of Olmeus Charles of Haiti and Borys Onyshchenko of the USSR. Charles took so long to finish his heat of the 10,000 Metres that he ran the last six laps all by himself. Onyshchenko, subsequently dubbed 'Dis-Onyshchenko', was disqualified from the Modern Pentathlon for using an epee with a built-in circuit-breaker enabling him to register a hit even when he hadn't made one.

(*Previous page*) British skiers at Sapporo, Japan for the Olympic Winter Games, 2 March 1972 – (from left to right) Valentina Iliffe, Carol Blackwood, Gina Hathorne, and Divina Galica.

WHAT A DIFFERENCE FOUR YEARS MAKE
(*Far left*) Mary Peters in action during the second day of the Women's Pentathlon, 3 September, 1972. She had finished ninth at Mexico, but won gold in Munich. The final discipline was the 200 Metres, which she finished, in her own words, 'with legs like jelly'. If she had run one tenth of a second slower, the gold medal would have gone to Heidemarie Rosendahl of Germany. (*Left above*) John Sherwood, who took bronze in the 400-Metre Hurdles at Mexico City, fails to qualify for the final in Munich.

A CLUTCH OF GOLD (*Bottom right*)
The British Three-Day Event team that won gold at the Munich Olympics – (left to right) Captain Mark Phillips, Mary Gordon Watson, Richard Meade, and Bridget Parker. (*Left below*) Brian Jacks grapples with Oh Seung-lip of Korea in the Middleweight Judo contest at Munich. Jacks won bronze, Seung-lip won silver. (*Top right*) The official poster designed by Victor Vaserely for the 1972 Munich Olympic Games.

CANADA
1976

IN LASSE VIREN'S FOOTSTEPS Brendan Foster (*left below*) fights his way through the 10,000 Metres in Montreal, July 1976. Ahead of him is Carlos Lopes of Portugal, but ahead of both of them is Lasse Viren, winning his second Olympic gold in this event. Lopes took silver, Foster took bronze. (*Left above*) The Maple Leaf stands proud on the poster for the Montreal Olympics.

BACK TO BARRACKS Sergeant Jim Fox stands in the back of a RMP Land Rover (*far left*), flanked by Mike Proudfoot (Team Manager) and Adrian Parker on his right, and Danny Nightingale and Andy Archibald on his left as they return to Aborfield Camp, Berkshire after winning gold in the Modern Pentathlon at Montreal, 4 August, 1976. It was Fox who solved the mystery of Boris Dis-Onyshchenko's magic, but illegal, epee.

OLYMPIC PEGASUS 'Hideaway', Graham Fletcher's mount for the Prix des Nations Jumping competition at the Montreal Olympics, is coaxed on to a plane at Gatwick Airport, 13 July, 1976 (*right*). Horse and team reached the last eight, but failed to win a medal in the face of superb performances by France, Germany, and Belgium.

ROYAL GROOM Captain Mark Phillips (*above*) pays some last minute attention to HRH Princess Anne's top hat before the dressage section of the Equestrian Three Day event at Montreal. Princess Anne once said: 'The horse is about the only person who does not know you are Royal.'

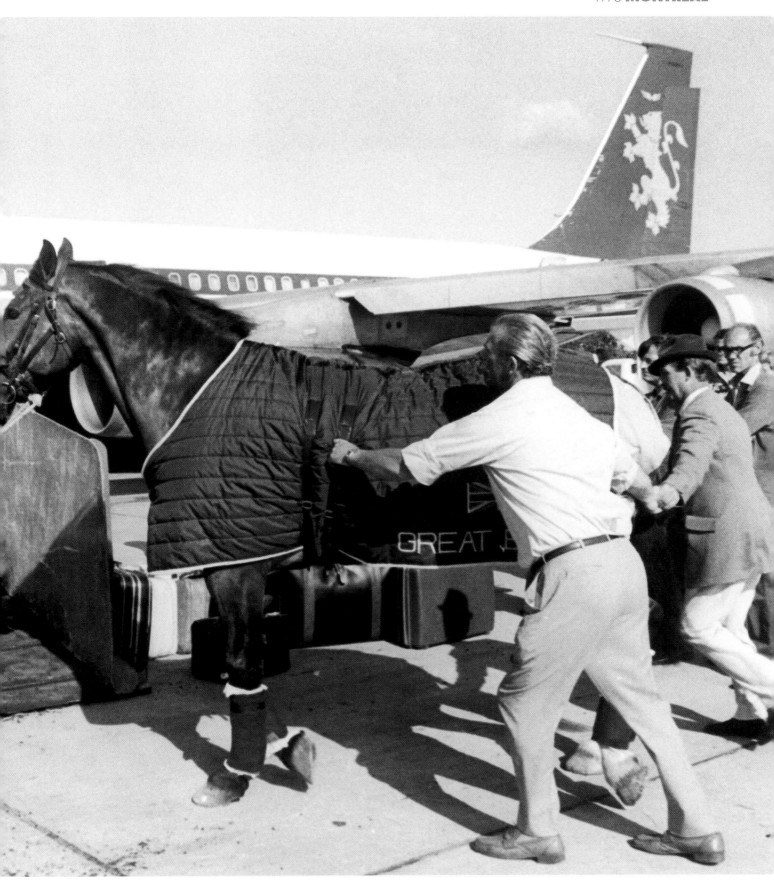

GLIDING TO GOLD John Curry (*left*) on the practice rink at Innsbruck for the 1976 Olympic Winter Games. His ability to combine the artistry of ballet with spectacular leaps brought him the gold medal in the Men's Figure Skating, despite disapproval from Eastern-bloc judges, some of whom believed that his style was 'too feminine'. Following his victory, Curry turned professional and moved to the United States, where he said the training facilities were better. (*Above*) The poster for the Innsbruck Games.

1980 MOSCOW LAKE PLACID
1984 LOS ANGELES SARAJEVO
1988 SEOUL CALGARY

All went well at the 1980 Olympic Winter Games at Lake Placid, where Robin Cousins failed to produce his best form yet took gold in the Men's Figure Skating, but the Summer Games in Moscow fell foul of yet another boycott. President Carter banned American athletes from the Games in protest at the alleged Soviet invasion of Afghanistan. Ordered by the British Government to do the same, the BOA dug in their heels, for they received no government subsidy and were truly independent. 'We had decided long ago,' said Sir Denis Follows, Chair of the BOA, 'that whether one went to the Olympic Games or not was solely a matter for the individual competitor to determine.' Tough campaigning by the BOA and individual athletes alike ensured that most Western European countries took a similar attitude.

The BOA raised £800,000 to pay for a British team to join those from the other 80 nations. It was Britain's best games since 1956, with five gold, seven silver, and nine bronze medals. The British Rowing Eight missed gold by three seconds. Allan Wells became the first British athlete to win the 100 Metres since Harold Abrahams at Paris in 1924, and missed out on gold in the 200 Metres by only 0.02 of a second. Sebastian Coe ran what he called 'the worst race of my life' to take second place to Steve Ovett in the 800-Metres Final. Daley Thompson stretched every muscle in his body to win gold in the Decathlon. Neil Adams won silver in the Judo Lightweight class, defeated by a man who had bitten him on the buttocks in the 1977 European Championships. There was gold for Duncan Goodhew in the 100-Metres Freestyle, and silver for Sharron Davies in the 400-Metre Individual Medley.

Four years later, on a tit-for-tat basis, the Soviet Union boycotted the Los Angeles Games. The XXIII Olympiad produced 37 medals for Britain and a debate over the gulf between Olympic and commercial cultures. The opening and closing ceremonies displayed Hollywood at its best and worst. One of the two Olympic Villages was situated in what was called 'poor and hostile country'. Zola Budd and Mary Decker clashed on the track. The TV coverage took the breath away.

Calgary hosted the Winter Games of 1988, at which Eddie 'The Eagle' Edwards gloriously re-affirmed the old amateur spirit of the Olympics. The XXIV Olympiad was held in Seoul, and a record 160 nations took part. The BOA raised the necessary £3 million and sent 386 competitors. Redgrave and Holmes won gold and bronze, Christie took two silvers. Adrian Moorhouse swam to victory, Malcolm Cooper shot his way to gold with a rifle repaired by a Soviet gunsmith. And, on 22 September, Britain won more medals in a single day than they had done for over 60 years.

MOSCOW 1980

(*Previous page*) Rocket Man enters the Los Angeles Coliseum during the opening ceremony for the Olympic Games, 28 July, 1984.

PLUNGING FROM THE HEIGHTS Deborah Jay of Great Britain (*above*) dives from the springboard into the pool at the Moscow Olympics, 20 July, 1980. The event was dominated by the USSR and the German Democratic Republic who, in the absence of divers from the United States, took the first five places. (*Left*) One of a series of posters for the Moscow Games. There were posters for each sport, but this was the more widely displayed generic design.

EMERGING FROM THE DEPTHS (*Far left*) Breaststroke swimmers Duncan Goodhew (left) and David Wilkie train together. Wilkie's great success had been at the Montreal Olympics, when he took gold in the 200 Metres and smashed the world record. Goodhew won the 100 Metres at Moscow. Despite all the noise in the swimming stadium, Goodhew claimed he could hear his mothers voice above all others, cheering him on.

SWAPPING PLACES The form book was upset at the Moscow Olympics by Britain's middle distance runners. Sebastian Coe was supposed to win the 800 Metres, but came second to Steve Ovett (*top left*), with Nicolai Kirov taking bronze. Steve Ovett was supposed to win the 1,500 Metres, but came third behind Sebastian Coe who won the gold (*below left*), and Jurgen Straub who took silver.

AN OUTSIDE CHANCE (*Above*) Allan Wells, on the left of the picture and in the outside lane, begins the forward lean that enabled him to win gold by some five centimetres in the 100 Metres. Wells changed from long-jumper to sprinter in 1976, and used starting blocks for the first time in the year he won Olympic gold. (*Left below*) British fans send a message to the Prime Minister. The Government mounted a strong campaign to dissuade athletes from going to Moscow. Wells received letters containing photographs of dead Afghan children.

NOTHING TO DO WITH THE TRAPPINGS…
Robin Cousins (*left*) at full stretch over the
ice at Lake Placid, New York, 21 February,
1980. Cousins took gold in the Men's Figure
Skating with a scintillating performance in
the XIII Winter Olympiad. As a child, his hero
had been the dancer Gene Kelly, but he took
up skating as his sport. Like Curry, Cousins
later turned professional. He later said that
success in sport had 'nothing to do with the
trappings', in that skill and dedication were
more important than the finest equipment.

NOT ALTOGETHER PLACID (*Above*) One of
the posters for the Lake Placid Olympic
Winter Games. The Games were boycotted
by Taiwan, in protest at the IOC's refusal to
allow their team to enter as the 'Republic of
China'. And the Games were considered an
'organisational disaster', with many tickets
remaining unsold even though fans wished to
buy them.

Games of the XXIIIrd Olympiad Los Angeles 1984

REDGRAVE'S FIRST The winning British team (*right*) in the Coxed Four event, at Lake Casitas during the Los Angeles Olympics, 5 August, 1984. The team are (from left to right) Martin Cross, Dr Richard Budgett (Team GB's current Chief Medical Officer), Andy Holmes, Steve Redgrave, and Adrian Ellison. The finish was dramatic, as the British boat emerged from the mist, with Redgrave heroically stroking it past the US team to win by less than two seconds. He went on to win gold medals in five successive Olympics.

'WHO SAYS I'M FINISHED!' Sebastian Coe (*above right*) hurls his challenge to the British press after his sensational victory in the 1,500 Metres at Los Angeles, while Steve Cram, who took silver, looks on. (*Above*) Tessa Sanderson breaks the Olympic record and wins gold in the Women's Javelin. She was the first British athlete to win gold in a throwing event. Fatima Whitbread took bronze in the same event. (*Left above*) An official poster for the XXIII Olympiad at Los Angeles.

THE MODERN PROMETHEUS (*Far left*) Daley Thompson clears 5.00 metres in the Pole Vault discipline of the Los Angeles Decathlon, 9 August, 1984. In so doing he more or less assured himself of gold. Daley scored 8,797 points, one point behind the world record. The photograph for the 110-Metres Hurdles was reread later and his time decreased by 0.01 of a second, giving him one more point to equal the world record.

All-ROUND BETTER PERFORMANCE In 1984, Thompson improved on his gold-medal winning performances at Moscow four years earlier in nearly every discipline. (*Clockwise from above*) Thompson clears 2.03 metres in the High Jump, celebrates his Pole Vault success with his famous back-flip, and stretches to 8.01 metres in the Long Jump.

SHEER PERFECTION Ravel's *Bolero* returns to its home key, and Christopher Dean and Jayne Torvill complete their Ice Dance routine in the Olympic Winter Games at Sarajevo in 1984 (*left*). It was an awe-inspiring performance that not only won them the gold medal, but also brought them unprecedented marks from the judges. The electronic scoreboard (*above*) registered 6.0 (sest-nula in Serbo-Croat) from all nine judges. (*Top*) One of the posters produced for the 1984 Olympic Winter Games in Sarajevo.

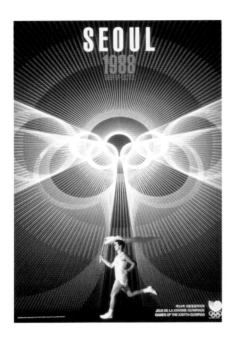

EASTERN PARADE For once there was no boycott, and a record 8,465 athletes took part in the 1988 Olympic Games at Seoul in South Korea. Following the pattern established at the Los Angeles Games, the Seoul opening ceremony was lavishly spectacular, and here (*right*) twirling pom-poms add colour and movement to the show. (*Above left*) One of the poster designs for the 1988 Seoul Olympics. (*Above right*) A young Olympic fan.

AGAINST THE ODDS Fatima Whitbread (*left*) had suffered from a trapped nerve in her throwing shoulder, a foot injury, hamstring problems, glandular fever, and an abscess in her back in the year before Seoul, but still managed to win the silver medal in the Women's Javelin.

BEFORE THE TEST (*Top right*) Ben Johnson (extreme left) raises his hand in premature celebration after covering 100 metres in 9.79 seconds. The next day he was disqualified for taking steroids, and the gold medal went to Carl Lewis (extreme right), with Linford Christie (third from left) taking silver, and Calvin Smith (second from left) taking bronze. (*Below right*) Mark Rowland (third from right) clears the water jump on his way to the silver medal in the 3,000-Metre Steeplechase, 30 September, 1988. (*Below far right*) Colin Jackson takes silver in the Men's 110-Metre Hurdles.

JUMPING FOR JOY For the first time since the Antwerp Games in 1920, Britain win gold in the Olympic Field Hockey event, Seoul, 1 October, 1988. In a display that combined attack with superb defensive play, the British team beat Germany 3–1 in the final. Sean Kerly (*left*) enjoys the moment. (*Right*) Imran Sherwani, scorer of two of Britain's three goals, slips between two German defenders.

HEADING FOR THE FINAL Members of the British team hurl themselves into a heap of joy after scoring a goal against Australia in the semi-final (*below*). It was a tense game with an unexpected result. Scores were tied at 2–2 until Sean Kerly scored with less than a minute and a half still to play, and no time for Australia to fight back.

REAL SKIING, ARTIFICIAL SNOW

The Alpine events at Calgary were held on artificial snow. (*Far right*) Martin Bell puts in the best performance to date for a British skier in the Men's Combined, with a time of 2:02:49. (*Right*) One of the posters for the Calgary Olympic Winter Games. (*Right centre and below*) Eddie 'The Eagle' Edwards competing in the Olympic Ski Jumping competition; and at a press conference. He achieved world fame as the first British competitor ever to compete in the sport.

1992 BARCELONA ALBERTVILLE
1994 LILLEHAMMER
1996 ATLANTA
1998 NAGANO

The world order changed. Apartheid came to an end in South Africa. The Berlin Wall was demolished. The Soviet Union collapsed, but there was still a Soviet team at the XXV Olympiad in Barcelona. Estonia, Lithuania, and Latvia returned as independent nations to the Olympic fold. The German team now came from a united Germany. For the first time in 20 years all nations were represented, though athletes from Yugoslavia were admitted only as 'independent Olympic participants' – they won a silver and two bronze medals.

With the BOA's resources all but drained by the three Olympics of the 1980s, the Sports Council, sponsorship and Lottery money now came to the rescue. On top of this, the BOA somehow managed to raise £2 million. There were many great moments in Barcelona in 1992: the debut of Chris Boardman's bike, Derek Redmond's gutsy heroism, Simon Terry's Individual Archery medal (Britain's first in that sport for 80 years), Garry Herbert's message to the Searle brothers at the half-way stage of the Coxed Pairs ('If not you, who? If not now, when?'), and Graham Brookhouse's proposal of marriage, live on radio. For the first time, professionals were allowed to take part. 'I think the time has come,' said Linford Christie, 'when we should be paid to compete at the Olympic Games.' At Barcelona, he was probably happy enough with his 100-Metre gold medal.

The 1992 Winter Games were held in Albertville, but now came a change in timetabling. Summer and Winter Games were staggered, so that the Lillehammer Winter Games were held in 1994. They produced two bronze medals – for Nicky Gooch in Speed Skating, and for Torvill and Dean in Ice Dance – and there was also a bronze for the British Four Man Bobsleigh team at Nagano in 1998.

The XXVI Olympiad brought 197 nations and 10,744 competitors to Atlanta in 1996 for the centenary of the Modern Games, the biggest ever staged and also the most commercial. The bus service from the Olympic Village to events was appalling – British rowers had to hijack the bus to reach Lake Lanier, 55 miles away, as the driver had no idea how to get there. The computerized results system failed repeatedly. A bomb exploded in the Centennial Olympic Park, killing one person and injuring over a hundred.

(*Previous page*) With Barcelona's famous Sagrada Familia in the background, a competitor practices for the Women's Platform Diving contest at the 1992 Olympics.

CARRYING THE FLAG Steve Redgrave (*above*) leads the British team into the Montjuic Stadium for the Opening Ceremony at the Barcelona Olympics, 25 July, 1992. He had already won gold at Los Angeles in 1984 and Seoul in 1988, but there was more gold and more Olympian effort ahead. (*Inset*) Perhaps the most widely known of the 58 different posters designed for the Barcelona Games.

THREE IN A ROW At the end of the Coxless Pairs at Barcelona, July 1992 (*left*), Steve Redgrave (*right*) and Matthew Pinsent acknowledge the cheers of team-mates and supporters. It was Redgrave's third gold in three successive Games, a feat previously achieved by only two other British Olympians – water polo players Paul Radmilovic and Charles Smith – 72 years earlier.

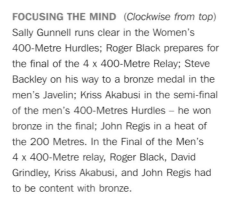

FOCUSING THE MIND (*Clockwise from top*)
Sally Gunnell runs clear in the Women's
400-Metre Hurdles; Roger Black prepares for
the final of the 4 x 400-Metre Relay; Steve
Backley on his way to a bronze medal in the
men's Javelin; Kriss Akabusi in the semi-final
of the men's 400-Metres Hurdles – he won
bronze in the final; John Regis in a heat of
the 200 Metres. In the Final of the Men's
4 x 400-Metre relay, Roger Black, David
Grindley, Kriss Akabusi, and John Regis had
to be content with bronze.

NOT ALL HEROES ARE WINNERS (*Right*)
This became one of the lasting and most
moving images of the Barcelona Olympics.
Derek Redmond is helped from the track by
his father. He had dedicated his performance
in the semi-final of the 400 Metres to his
father, but 150 metres into the race, he tore
a hamstring. Unable to run, he hobbled on,
in intense pain. His father shooed officials
away, and supported Redmond while they
finished the lap together, to a standing
ovation. Redmond's coach, Tony Handley,
cried when he saw the bonding between
father and son, 'I cried because he had
epitomized the Olympic spirit and
transcended the event.'

THE 100 METRE RAINBOW Wrapped in the Union Jack, Linford Christie (*left*) savours the joy of his victory in the 100 Metres at the Montjuïc Stadium, Barcelona, 1 August, 1992. At 32, Christie was the oldest athlete by four years to win the most coveted of Olympic gold medals. His time was 0.01 of a second faster than he had run to win silver at Seoul. It was perhaps the greatest moment in his career.

OVERTAKING AT THE NINTH Sally Gunnell (*above*) was trailing Sandra Farmer-Patrick as the runners went into the final bend of the Women's 400-Metre Hurdles Final at Barcelona. The American's rhythm was thrown when she clipped the seventh hurdle, however, and Gunnell seized her chance. She shot past at the ninth hurdle to win by three and a half metres and take gold.

TAKING COVER (*Left*) Jane Sixsmith (on left) takes evasive action during the semi-final of the Women's Hockey against Germany. Though Britain lost this match, they went on to beat Korea 4–3 in the play-off, and thus won a bronze medal.

ENTER THE ADVANCED COMPOSITE MONOCOQUE (*Above*) Chris Boardman on his way to gold in the Men's 4,000-Metre Individual Pursuit. His revolutionary bike caused a sensation at Barcelona.

A WEALTH OF EXPERIENCE (*Far left*) Graham Bell skims down the steep mountain course in the Men's Downhill at 1992 Albertville Olympic Winter Games. Bell participated in five consecutive Olympics. (*Top above*) Mark Tout and Lenox Paul hurtle down the Two-Man Bobsleigh course – at the halfway stage of the competition they were lying first. (*Above*) World Champion Wilf O'Reilly corners in the Men's 1,000-Metre Speed Skating. (*Left*) The official poster for the 1992 Olympic Winter Games, held at Albertville, France.

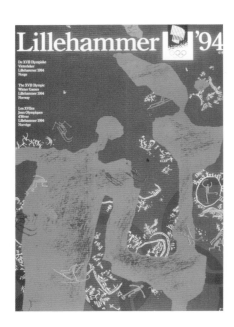

FINGER TIP CORNERING (*Right*) Nicky Gooch (third from left) keeps up the pressure in the Men's 500-Metre Short Track Speed Skating semi-final at the Lillehammer Olympic Winter Games, 22 February, 1994. Gooch reached the final and took the bronze medal in this event, part of the revival of British success in the Winter Games during the last 15 years. At the same Games, Torvill and Dean (*inset*) also won bronze in the Ice Dance category, though they felt their performance was better received by the audience than the judges. (*Above*) One of the official posters for the Lillehammer Games.

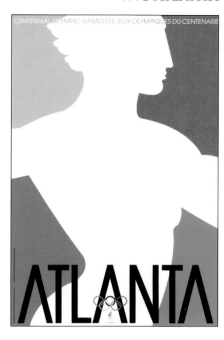

NEXT TIME AROUND... Jonathan Edwards (*far left*) hops, steps, and jumps his way to a silver medal in the Triple Jump at the Atlanta Games, 26th July, 1996. He was already the record holder, but couldn't quite reproduce his best at this Olympics, and Kenny Harrison beat Edwards by 21 centimetres. (*Centre*) Denise Lewis finished third in the Women's Heptathlon. Four years later, she was to add over a metre and a half to the length of her shot put with ecstatic results. (*Left above*) Neil Broad (left) and Tim Henman share a 'high-five' on their way to silver in the Men's Doubles. (*Left below*) Sharon Rendle of Great Britain (right) battles with Lynda Mekzine of Algeria in the Women's 63kg Class Judo. (*Above*) The official poster at the Atlanta Games.

REPEAT PERFORMANCE (*Overleaf*) Matthew Pinsent and Steve Redgrave power their way through to yet another gold medal in the Coxless Pairs. It was Redgrave's fourth gold medal in four consecutive Olympics.

A BATTLE AT SEA The final of the Laser Class sailing event at Savannah, during the Atlanta Games, became a struggle between Robert Scheidt of Brazil and Ben Ainslie (*overleaf inset*) of Great Britain. Scheidt led by two points going into the final race. Such was the intensity of the rivalry, both men were disqualified for false starts, leaving Scheidt with gold and Ainslie with silver.

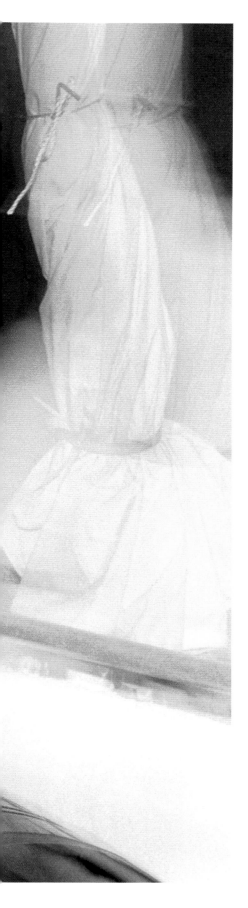

SECOND COUSINS (*Top left*) Steven Cousins leaves the ice during his routine in the Men's Figure Skating competition at the Nagano Olympic Winter Games in Japan, 14 February, 1998. (*Below left*) Masuteru Aoba's poster showing a thrush perching on a ski pole, selected as the official poster for the Nagano Olympic Winter Games.

BUILDING A NEW TEAM The British Four Man Bobsleigh team (*far left*) puts on the brakes at the end of their bronze medal winning run in the Nagano Olympic Winter Games, 21 February, 1998. The team consisted of Dean Ward, Courtney Rumbolt, Paul Attwood, and the driver, Sean Olsson. 'Every time before I go down,' said Olsson, 'I feel on edge… that never goes away.' They were the first British medal winners in this event since the 1936 Olympics.

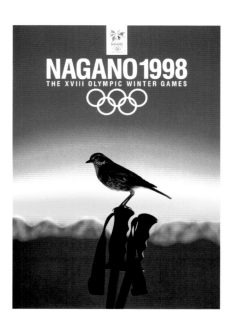

NAGANO 1998
THE XVIII OLYMPIC WINTER GAMES

2000 SYDNEY
2002 SALT LAKE CITY
2004 ATHENS

Some 60 years ago, in an essay called 'The Sporting Spirit', George Orwell wrote that 'sport is war without the shooting.' Perhaps the greatest achievement of the Olympic Movement has been to prove gloriously that Orwell was wrong. In the 1896 Olympiad, 14 nations took part and 245 competitors shared 123 medals. Overall, each athlete was entering with a 50 per cent chance of medal success. When the Games returned to Athens in 2004, where 11,099 athletes from 202 nations shared 929 medals, that chance was now 8 per cent. An Olympic Marathon runner once remarked: 'It is some cheek to aim at a gold medal… you're saying, "I am better than all the other 2.5 billion people in the world."' Cynics might suggest that there would be far less expense and far less work for all concerned if only the world's eight best teams or contestants in each event were invited. Why bother with heats and semi-finals and also-rans? Cut to the chase, create a final by picking the best and letting them get on with it.

But in the Olympics, commitment is not the monopoly of the winner. All those who take part are determined to outdo their previous best, no matter how far behind the winners that still leaves them. Before taking part in a swimming final, David Davies said to his coach: 'If I drop dead during the race, just come and fish me out'. At Athens, when another rider crashed into the back of Marc Jenkins' bike in the Triathlon, he picked it up and set off on foot in sweltering heat for the next wheel change point, two kilometres away. He was given a standing ovation when he finished last. After driving his canoe through the 500-Metres K1 Final in constant agony from an injured ankle, Ian Wynne explained: 'It never crossed my mind to pull out.'

In the 1896 Olympiad 14 nations took part. At the 'Welcome Home' Games in Athens in 2004, athletes and officials from 202 nations assembled. The torch that lit the Olympic Flame on 11 August had been carried around the world. Over the next 18 days, athletes competed in 37 different sports – among them many that didn't exist in de Coubertin's day. For Britain, Athens was a triumphant return to the birthplace of the Modern Games, with 30 medals, covering everything from Archery to Yngling, from Boxing to the Madison. There were golds in the Men's 4 x 100-Metre Relay, and in the Equestrian Three Day Team event. Ben Ainslie won a second Sailing gold. Kelly Holmes won gold in the 800 and 1,500 Metres. There were golds in both Men's and Women's Rowing.

And perhaps de Coubertin's successor, the Comte de Baillet-Latour, was right: when the Olympic flag flies over a stadium, a field, a stretch of water, a snow-covered piste, an ice rink, or a boxing ring, we are indeed in another country, where fairer rules apply.

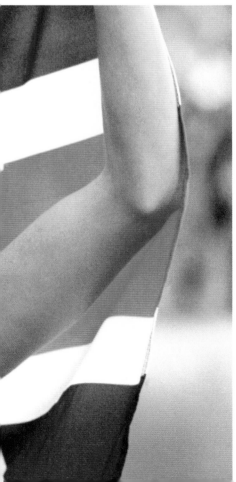

(*Previous page*) British cyclists in the 4,000-Metre Team Pursuit event at the Sydney Olympics ride wheel to wheel in the Dunc Gray Velodrome, Bankstown, 18 September, 2000.

SHOWING THE FLAG Jonathan Edwards (*far left, top*) forgets the disappointment of Atlanta and celebrates winning gold in the Triple Jump at Sydney, 25 September, 2000. (*Far left, below*) Steph Cook (right) and Kate Allenby wrap themselves in the flag after respectively winning gold and bronze medals in the Women's Modern Pentathlon at Sydney. Cook saved the best for last, and only one athlete came within 50 seconds of her time in the final discipline, the 3,000 Metres.

FLAT OUT, DOWN UNDER (*Left, clockwise from bottom*) Darren Campbell storms through a heat of the 100 Metres, 22 September, 2000. His success came two hours later, when he won a surprise silver in the 200 Metres. The official poster for the Sydney Games. Denise Lewis comes in second in the 100-Metre Hurdles leg of the Women's Heptathlon – she went on to win gold in the overall event.

(*Overleaf*) Audley Harrison punches his way a step nearer the gold medal in his Super-Heavyweight quarter-final fight with Oleskii Mazikin, 27 September, 2000.

WATERBORNE SUCCESS Team GB enjoyed itself on the water at Sydney, with yet another Redgrave gold (*top right*), this time shared between (from left to right) Tim Foster, Matthew Pinsent, Steve Redgrave, and James Cracknell in the Coxless Fours. There were five yachting medals: gold for Ben Ainslie in the Laser class, Iain Percy in the Finn class, and for Shirley Robertson in the Europe class; silver for Ian Walker and Mark Covell in the Star class, and for Ian Barker and Simon Hiscocks (*centre*) in the 49er class. And on dry land (*right below*) Richard Faulds took gold in the Men's Double Trap Shooting, 20 September, 2000.

VICTORY LAP (*Left*) Jason Queally cruises round the Dunc Gray Velodrome, Bankstown after winning gold in the final of the Men's 1,000-Metre Time Trial on the opening day of the 2000 Sydney Olympics, 16 September, 2000. Before the Olympics, Queally had cursed himself for his late start in cycling, saying: 'If I'd started at the age of 12 or 13, I could have been an Olympic champion.'

HIGHS AND LOWS AT SALT LAKE CITY
(*Right, clockwise from top left*) For the third
Games running, biathlete Michael Dixon
carries the flag at the opening of the 2002
Olympic Winter Games. The Olympic flag flies
on the official poster for the Games. Alain
Baxter produces the finest performance by a
British skier in the history of the Olympic
Winter Games. He was placed third in the
Men's Slalom, to win Britain's first skiing
medal, but two days later he tested positive
for a banned substance. This was a tragedy,
the result of using a brand of nasal inhaler
that was harmless in Britain but contained a
banned substance in its American form.
(*Opposite, left*) Alex Coomber lifts off as she
takes to the ice in training for the Women's
Skeleton event at the Peaks Ice Arena in
Provo, Utah, 19 February, 2002. She later
took the bronze medal in this event.

A SWEEPING SUCCESS (*Bottom right*)
Team captain Rhona Martin (centre) releases
the stone during the final of the Women's
Curling competition at the Salt Lake City
Games, 21 February, 2002. Martin, Janice
Rankin, Fiona MacDonald, Debbie Knox, and
Margaret Morton, the Scottish 'housewives'
as they were dubbed, defeated Switzerland
with the last sweep of the broom to give
Britain gold for the first time in this event.

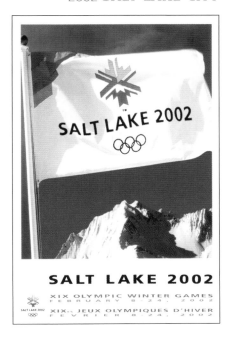

FOUR IN A BOAT, FOUR IN A ROW

The Men's Coxless Fours brought Matthew Pinsent his fourth gold medal in successive Olympics. Crowned with their laurel wreaths after their photo-finish success (*far right*), James Cracknell puts his arm round a tearful Pinsent while Ed Coode looks on, 21 August, 2004. (*Top left*) Campbell Walsh fights white water on his way to a silver medal in the men's K1 class Kayaking competition. (*Top right*) The official emblem for the Athens 2004 Olympic Games. (*Above*) Ben Ainslie steers his way to gold in the Finn class sailing event, 21 August, 2004.

DELIGHT, DISMAY AND DISBELIEF

Kelly Holmes' face says it all (*top left*) after her victory in the 800 Metres at the Olympic Stadium, 23 August, 2004. Five days later, she became the first British athlete to repeat Albert Hill's feat of 1920 in winning both 800 and 1,500 Metres. 'I can't believe it,' she said. 'I'm gobsmacked!' For Paula Radcliffe (*below left*) there was double dismay. Following her disappointment in the Marathon, she had to pull out of the 10,000 Metres, to stand by the trackside and watch the others pass by.

HOPPING AND JUMPING FOR JOY

Seconds after hitting the tape, Mark Lewis-Francis (*above left*) shows his joy at completing the victory set up by his team mates Jason Gardener, Darren Campbell, and Marlon Devonish in the Men's 4 x 100-Metre Relay. It was a gold against the odds. (*Above centre*) Kelly Sotherton hits High Jump happiness in the Women's Heptathlon, 20 August, 2004. She went on to take bronze. (*Above right*) Nathan Robertson and Gail Emms win a spectacular silver in the finals of the Mixed Doubles Badminton, 19 August, 2004.

FAIR SAILING Sarah Webb, Shirley Robertson, and Sarah Ayton enjoy their success after wining gold in the Women's Yngling class at the Agios Kosmas Olympic Sailing Centre, Athens, 21 August, 2004.

BACK WHERE IT ALL BEGAN The Archery events at the 2004 Olympics were held in the Panathinaiko Stadium, home of the Ancient Games and birthplace of the Modern Games in 1896. Alison Williamson (*far left top*) became the first British woman to win a medal in this event since Queenie Newall, Lottie Dod, and Beatrice Hill-Lowe at London in 1908. (*Far left below*) 17-year-old Amir Khan lashes out at Jong Sub Baik of Korea in the Lightweight Boxing quarter-final, 24 August, 2004. 'If anyone can, Khan can,' they chanted, and he went on to win silver.

FLYING HOOVES, WHIRLING WHEELS (*Top above*) Bradley Wiggins tears up the Velodrome on his way to gold in the Men's Individual Pursuit at the Olympic Sports Complex, Athens, 20 August, 2004. There were other medals to come. (*Left below*) Leslie Law on 'Shear l'Eau' leave the water on their way to gold in the Individual Three Day Event. Pippa Funnell on 'Primmore's Pride' took the bronze medal in the same event.

Peter Waterfield (right) and Leon Taylor head for silver in the Men's Synchronised Diving 10-Metre Platform event, 14 August, 2004. 'I was so fired up that I went a little early,' said Waterfield. 'And I didn't catch him up,' said Taylor.

INDEX

ACKNOWLEDGEMENTS

The book was created and printed by Getty Images Publishing Projects who wish to thank the team at the British Olympic Association including Simon Clegg, whose inspiration it was to create Chasing Gold, *Ann Blake, Phil Bolton, and Philip Pope.*

Getty Images has over 70 million images, and its sports coverage is justifiably renowned for both contemporary coverage as well as rare archival images. Matthew Eades, Neil Loft, Adrian Murrell, and Ian Buchanan all lent their vast knowledge of the Games and their discriminating eye to the task. Fernando Scippa of the International Olympic Committee also deserves special thanks.

Nick Yapp was a masterful researcher and author. Both Tea McAleer and Vivienne Brar's superb sense of design is evident throughout these pages, and Jennifer Jeffrey did a spectacular job seeking out wonderful images whilst Mark Fletcher edited and managed.

The International Olympic Comittee provided images on pages: 12–13, 14–15, 40, 149tr, 153br, 163tr, 164tr.

All other illustrations are courtesy of Getty Images' special collections held by or represented by Getty Images. Those requiring further attribution are indicated as follows: AFP: 117t, 118-119; Scott Barbour: 158–159; Al Bello: 171b; Shaun Botterill: 3, 137tr, 146–147, 152, 165, 172–173; Clive Brunskill: 1, 153tr, 163m; Simon Bruty: 130t, 131, 135, 136–137, 138tl, 141, 144; David Cannon: 127, 130b, 133, 143; Chris Cole: 142, 145m; John Dominis/Time & Life Pictures: 100; Tony Duffy: 101m, 110-111, 120b, 122, 123t, 123bl, 128, 129br, 138bm, 140, 148l; Darren England: 156t; Stu Forster: 157b, 166t, 167m; Stuart Franklin: 164tl; Sean Garnsworthy: 166b; Ernst Haas: 92-93; Mike Hewitt: 138tr, 156b, 161t, 161b, 163b; IOC Olympic Museum Collections : 11t, 13r, 14l, 19r, 34-37, 41, 45r, 49b, 51, 54-55, 57, 58b, 59, 61tr, 67tl, 71r, 77b, 79b, 80t, 83tr, 83br, 87r, 92l, 94l, 98l, 101t, 105tr, 107t, 111r, 115b, 119r, 120tl, 125tr, 126l, 132t, 137tl, 145b, 146tl; Ross Kinnaird: 149b, 160; Ron Kuntz/AFP: 129t; Andy Lyons: 157tr; Chris McGrath: 170b; Bob Martin: 138bl, 138br, 145t; Clive Mason: 164b, 168-169; Donald Miralle: 162, 163tl, 171t; Gray Mortimore: 129bl, 132m, 139; Mike Powell: 126r, 155; Steve Powell: 113, 120tr, 123br, 125br, 146tr; Adam Pretty: front cover; Gary M.Prior: 148r, 149tl; Pascal Rondeau: 150-151; Ezra Shaw: 161m; Jamie Squire: endpapers, 170t; Michael Steele: 167l; Ian Waldie: 167r; Nick Wilson: 157tl.